Magic Tricks
from the Tree House

MAGIC TREE HOUSE®

Magic Tricks
from the Tree House

A Fun Companion to
Magic Tree House #50: *Hurry Up, Houdini!*

by Mary Pope Osborne and Natalie Pope Boyce
illustrated by Sal Murdocca

A STEPPING STONE BOOK™
Random House 🏠 New York

With love to Carl and Gilbert Casey,
two magical tricksters

With many thanks to Jack Desroches, magician and
friend extraordinaire, for his help
and advice in preparing this book

Visit us on the Web!
MagicTreeHouse.com
randomhouse.com/kids

Educators and librarians, for a variety of teaching tools, visit us at
RHTeachersLibrarians.com

Library of Congress Cataloging-in-Publication Data
Osborne, Mary Pope.
Magic tricks from the tree house : a fun companion to magic tree house #50: hurry up,
Houdini! / Mary Pope Osborne and Natalie Pope Boyce ; illustrated by Sal Murdocca.
p. cm. — (Magic tree house)
ISBN 978-0-449-81790-2 (pbk.) — ISBN 978-0-449-81791-9 (lib. bdg.) —
ISBN 978-0-449-81792-6 (ebook)
[1. Magic tricks—Juvenile literature.] I. Murdocca, Sal, illustrator.
II. Title.
GV1548.O73 2013 793.8—dc23 2013007916

Printed in the United States of America

10 9 8 7 6 5 4 3 2 1

Random House Children's Books supports the First Amendment
and celebrates the right to read.

Contents

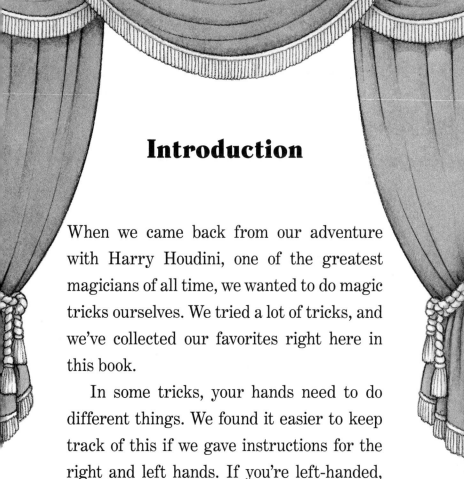

Introduction

When we came back from our adventure with Harry Houdini, one of the greatest magicians of all time, we wanted to do magic tricks ourselves. We tried a lot of tricks, and we've collected our favorites right here in this book.

In some tricks, your hands need to do different things. We found it easier to keep track of this if we gave instructions for the right and left hands. If you're left-handed, you can reverse the hands in the instructions to work better for you.

It's so much fun to be a magician! The best thing is that you learn to do awesome magic tricks for your friends and family. The second-best thing is that many of the tricks aren't very hard to do.

You don't have to be like Houdini, who made an elephant *seem* to disappear from the stage. You can learn easy tricks, and if you do them well, people will really enjoy them.

Start Simple

Every magician begins by learning basic tricks. But remember: they aren't really magic. The Great Houdini himself said that no one has magical powers, and you won't, either. Good magicians just make people think they do.

Practice, Practice, Practice!

Magicians have to be confident. You've got to know your tricks backward and forward. If you are unsure and fumble, you won't look cool. You'll just look confused.

To avoid this, you need to practice a lot. One of the best ways to practice is to perform your trick in front of a mirror until you can do it perfectly. Do the trick twenty times or thirty times or more! You could also record a video of yourself to watch for rough spots in your performance. Remember to write down tips for how to do the tricks in a notebook!

When you think you're ready, put on a show for your friends or family. Ask them if they see any problems in your act. Also ask them what you need to do to improve.

Patter

Magicians entertain the audience with *patter* throughout their acts. Patter is the talking that they do, and it's a big part of their acts. It keeps people interested and also keeps them from looking too closely at how the magician is doing a trick.

For example, you might begin your trick by saying "People all over the world have tried this trick, and *no one* has ever been able to do it. Ladies and gentlemen, what you see today will amaze you!"

Patter makes people focus on what you're saying rather than on what you're doing. It's a lot easier to fool your audience this way.

And don't forget to smile and have a really great time, too. Tell a few jokes. A serious magician isn't much fun.

Misdirection

Good magicians use a technique called *misdirection*. It's a way to keep people from looking too carefully at what your hands are up to. If your right hand is doing a secret move, stare hard at your left. People will automatically look where you look. You don't want to call attention to how you're doing something.

Dress the Part

If you want to be a magician, you need to look and act like one. Dress nicely. People will be looking at your hands, so make sure they're super clean.

If your props are a light color, such as a white napkin or tablecloth, it's a good idea to wear a darker shirt so that people can see them more easily. You can even wear a costume, maybe one with some pockets big enough to hold things for your act. A cool hat and cloak just might do the trick!

Props

A magician needs *props*, which are objects used in a performance. Your props don't have to be fancy. And they don't have to cost a lot of money.

For the tricks in this book, you'll use things that you can usually find around the house, like pencils, cards, drinking glasses, and handkerchiefs. It's also good to have a special stick or wand. You can wave it over your props as you chant "magic" words. And for most of the tricks, you'll need a small table.

The Rules
There are two big rules all magicians follow. The first is to never do the same trick twice during a show. Someone will probably figure it out the second time.

The second rule is to never tell anyone how you do a trick. Magicians like to pretend they're in a secret club. It's against club rules to reveal the tricks of the trade. And besides, if your secrets get out, every kid will become a magician and you'll lose your audience!

1

Steal-the-Strength Trick

OBJECT: Make a person seem to suddenly lose all strength.

What You Need:
- a volunteer from the audience who's about your size
- one of your fingers!

1. Call for a volunteer to come onstage, and ask him to try to lift you off the ground.

2. After the volunteer puts you back down, announce that if you touch a special spot under his chin it'll be impossible for him to pick you up again. Claim that by touching the spot, you'll be able to steal all his strength and transfer it to yourself.

3. Touch several places under the volunteer's chin as if you are trying to decide where the special spot is. Frown a little bit as you do this, and then smile when you "find" it.

4. Ask the volunteer to grab both your upper arms. Then tell him to try to lift you.

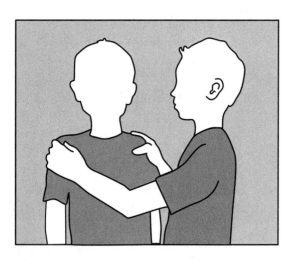

5. Keep your finger underneath his chin, and as he starts to pick you up, carefully and gently push his head up and back with your finger, saying "Give me your strength!" Keep gently pushing, and if you get your timing right, it'll be impossible for him to lift you!

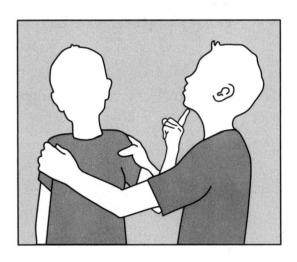

TRACKING THE FACTS:

When you gently push someone's chin up and back, it puts him off balance, and he can't lift you.

2

The Disappearing Paper Clip

OBJECT: Make a paper clip seem to evaporate!

What You Need:
- paper clip
- small but fairly strong magnet
- long-sleeved shirt with cuffs that fit snugly, to wear at the show

PREPARATION: Before you go onstage, prepare your shirt. Hide the magnet in the cuff of one of your sleeves. Make sure you have the active side of the magnet facing down. Your cuff should be tight enough to hold the magnet in place. If not, tape it to the inside of your cuff.

1. Say you'll make the paper clip disappear just by waving your hands over it.

2. Wave both hands over the clip, making them cross each other while saying "Paper clip, get thee gone! Disappear and vanish!" Keep the sleeve with the magnet in it on the bottom. Move your hands right above the clip so that they're almost touching it.

FACT: This type of trick is called a <u>gimmick</u>. A gimmick is when a hidden prop, like the magnet, makes the trick work.

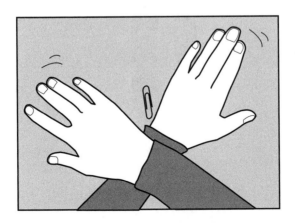

3. The paper clip should cling to the bottom of your sleeve.

4. Slowly uncross your hands, and announce in a dramatic voice that the paper clip has vanished!

3

Magical Clinging Pen

OBJECT: Make a pen "magically" cling to your hand.

What You Need:
- pen, pencil, or ruler

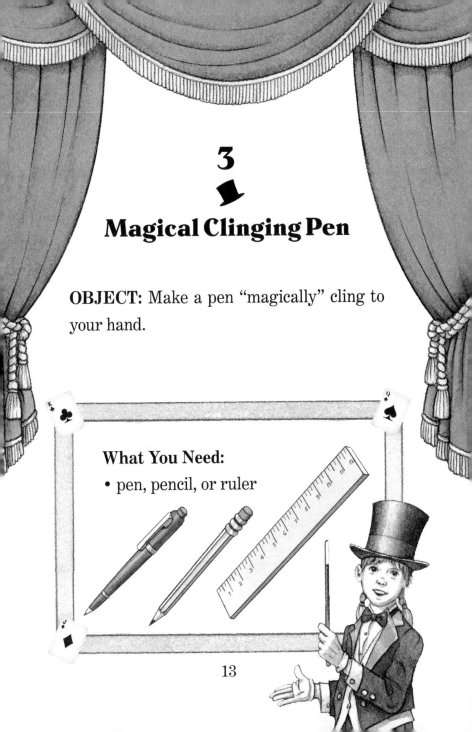

TIP:
Be
organized!
Make a
prop list
in a
notebook.
List props
you need
for all your
tricks so
you won't
forget
anything.

1. Hold your left hand out, palm down.

2. Announce that you can produce your own electricity. Begin by rubbing the pen (or pencil or ruler) up and down your left arm as if you are creating static electricity. As you do this, mutter to yourself, "Yes, I feel the charge getting stronger by the minute."

3. Put the pen in your left hand, and close your left fist to grip it.

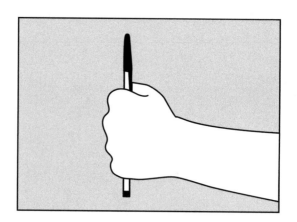

4. With your right palm facing up, grab your left wrist with your right hand.

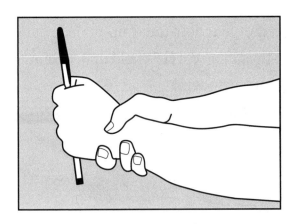

5. Using the pointer (index) finger of your right hand, secretly hold the pen in place. Spread out the fingers and thumb on your left hand, so the audience can see all five fingers. Keep your right index finger on the pen.

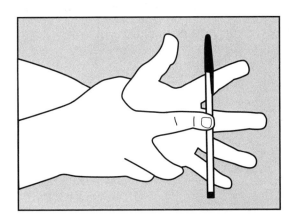

6. Shake your left hand up and down. The pen stays in place! (It's held up by your right finger, remember?)

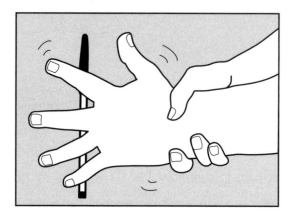

7. Finish the trick by closing your left hand and taking your right hand off your left wrist. Finally turn your left palm up and give the pen to an audience member, saying "This magic pen is just for you."

4

The Great Pepper Trick

OBJECT: Make pepper move across water.

What You Need:
- liquid hand soap or dish soap
- drinking glass
- water
- shaker of black pepper
- paper towel to wipe off the volunteer's hands

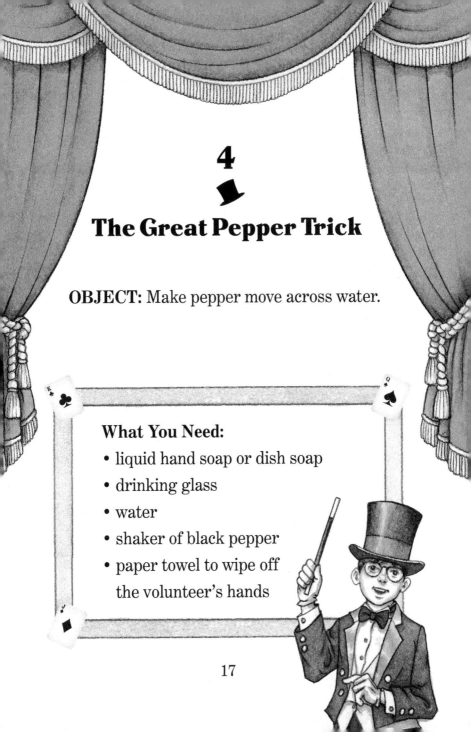

1. Before the show, rub soap on the tips of both of your pointer fingers.

2. Fill the glass with water and put it on the table.

3. As the audience watches, sprinkle pepper in the water. (Practice a few times to figure out how much pepper works best.) Then say that only *your* magic finger can make the pepper move to the edge of the glass.

4. Call on a volunteer to come up to the table.

5. Ask the volunteer to put her hand in the water. The pepper will stick to her hand.

6. Put your soapy finger in the water. Chant something like "Pepper, obey what I say! Get to the edge of the glass!" The pepper will move to the edge, just as you told it to!

7. For fun, you can ask another volunteer to come up and try it. The pepper will stick to his hand, too. Then add more pepper and do the trick with your other soapy finger. Yippee! The pepper moves on your command!

TRACKING THE FACTS:

When water comes into contact with air, the surface holds together, almost as if it's covered by a thin layer of skin or plastic. This is called <u>surface tension</u>. When soap mixes into the water, it breaks the surface tension of the water, which allows the water to spread and take the pepper with it.

5

The Cool and Slightly
Gross Thumb Trick

OBJECT: Make it look as if you're pulling off your right thumb with your left hand. This really takes practice, so be patient.

What You Need:

- nothing but your hands!

1. Hold your hands chest high. Your left hand should be straight up, with the palm facing the audience.

2. Your right hand should be horizontal, with the palm facing your chest.

3. Bend your right thumb.

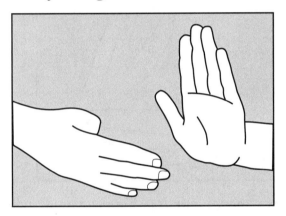

4. Bend your left thumb, and bend the pointer finger of your left hand to cover the joint.

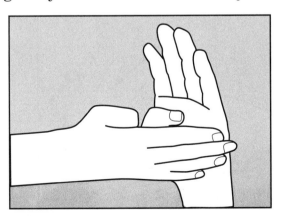

5. Make the joints of both thumbs touch each other. The pointer finger of your right hand will hide the place where the two thumbs meet and make it look as though they're just one thumb on your right hand.

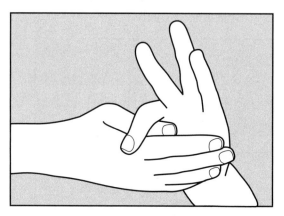

6. Slowly move your left hand away. It will look as if your thumb has detached from your right hand!

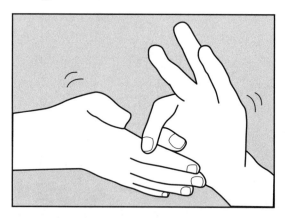

7. Do this a few times. Clap your hands, and it's finished!

6

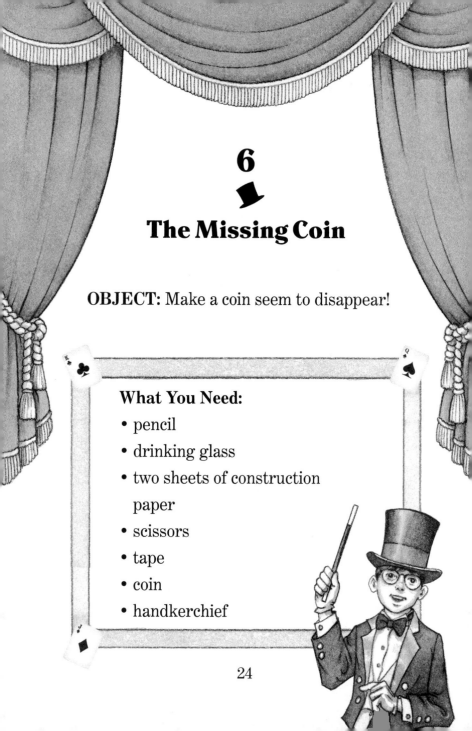

The Missing Coin

OBJECT: Make a coin seem to disappear!

What You Need:
- pencil
- drinking glass
- two sheets of construction paper
- scissors
- tape
- coin
- handkerchief

24

PREPARATION: With a pencil, trace a circle around the mouth of the glass onto a sheet of paper. Cut out the circle that you've traced and tape it to the mouth of the glass. Put a whole piece of the same colored paper on the table. Place the coin and the glass next to each other on the paper. The glass should be paper-side down. Since the paper on the glass is the same color as the paper on the table, the audience won't know you've covered the mouth of the glass. It will look like a regular upside-down glass.

FACT: Houdini's real name was Ehrich Weisz. It's more exciting to say the Great Houdini than the Great Ehrich, don't you think?

1. Place the handkerchief over the glass. Tell the audience that you'll instantly make the coin disappear.

2. Move the glass until the paper that's on it covers the coin. Remember to patter away while you're doing this.

3. Say a few magic words, wave your hand, and pull off the handkerchief. The coin is

25

gone! (Of course, the coin is really there, underneath the paper that is covering the mouth of the glass.)

7

Knotted Rope Trick

OBJECT: Make a knot appear like magic at the end of a rope.

What You Need:
* piece of rope, about three feet long

TIP:
Think of
a great
stage
name to
use when
you
perform.

PREPARATION: Before the show, tie a big knot at one end of the rope. Keep it on the floor behind the table so the audience can't see it.

1. Pick up the rope and hide the knotted end in one hand. Grab the other end of the rope with your other hand and put it in the hand with the hidden knot.

2. Show both closed hands to the audience. Announce that you can make a knot appear in the rope without tying it.

3. Shake your hands as if you are trying really hard to tie a knot. Maybe groan and mutter, "This is really, really tough . . . wonder if I can do it."

4. Then dramatically drop the end of the rope with the knot in it. You could finish by saying "Wow! I did it!" You might also invite the audience to inspect the rope.

8

Rising and Sinking Ketchup Packet

OBJECT: Make a packet of ketchup sink or float in a bottle when you cast a magic spell over it.

What You Need:

- ketchup packet
- water
- plastic soft drink or water bottle with an opening big enough to squeeze a ketchup packet through. Bottle should have a cap.

TIP:
There are magic clubs for kids in many towns and cities that you can join.

PREPARATION: Test your ketchup packet to make sure it will float. (Some packets float better than others.)

1. Pour water in the bottle, leaving an inch or so free at the top. Fold the ketchup packet in half carefully and push it into the bottle. Remember: it's supposed to float. It doesn't have to float on top of the water. It'll most likely float around the middle of the bottle.

2. Put the cap on the bottle, and without making a big deal of it, squeeze the bottle. Wave your other hand around to distract the audience and mutter, "May the power of Houdini be with me." The ketchup will sink to the bottom. To bring it back up, stop squeezing!

TRACKING THE FACTS:

The ketchup packet has an air bubble in it. This keeps it from sinking to the bottom. When you squeeze the bottle, the bubble gets smaller and the packet sinks. When you stop squeezing, the bubble gets larger and the packet floats.

9

The Big Color Trick

OBJECT: Guess the color of a crayon without looking at it.

What You Need:
- four crayons with distinct colors, such as yellow, blue, red, and green
- scarf to use as blindfold

1. Claim that you can tell the color of a crayon just by using your fantastic mental powers.

2. Put all four crayons on the table.

3. Ask a volunteer to blindfold you and then to put just one crayon in your hand.

4. Turn your back to the audience.

5. Move the crayon around in your hands. As you do this, scrape a bit of color off with a fingernail.

6. Take off the blindfold and give the crayon back to the volunteer.

7. Turn around; put your hand up to your head as if you are thinking. Then take a quick glance at your fingers to see what color you scraped off with your nail. Close your eyes and say something like, "Just a minute—it's the color of the sky" (blue) or "I see a park with lots of trees" (green). Pause, open your eyes, and call out the color.

FACT: Every three years, there's a world championship for magicians. The winner gets the International Federation of Magic Societies Grand Prix award.

10

The Hopping Rubber Band

OBJECT: "Magically" move a rubber band from one set of fingers to another.

What You Need:

- One medium-sized rubber band that will fit around your fingers but not be too tight or too loose. Try several different sizes until you find the right one.

1. Tell the audience that with your powerful magic, a rubber band will magically hop from finger to finger. With your palm facing you, put the rubber band around your ring and pinkie fingers and show the audience.

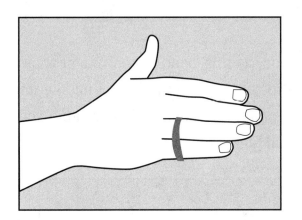

2. Keeping the band on your fingers, stretch it out to prove that it's all in one piece. Say something like, "See, ladies and gentlemen, this isn't a trick band—it's a normal rubber band. It just needs a little magic."

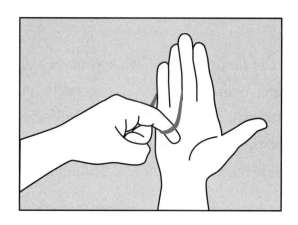

3. As you say this, bend all your fingers down and slip the band around your middle and index fingers. It should still be around your ring and pinkie fingers, too.

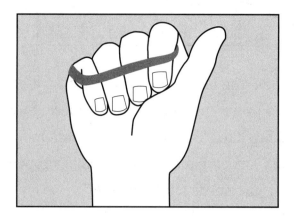

4. Rest your four fingers against the palm of your hand. The back of your hand should

still face the audience, and the band should be across your fingertips, not at your knuckles. The audience shouldn't see that you've added extra fingers.

5. Now say, "Watch closely . . . sometimes the hand is quicker than the eye. With an ordinary rubber band and my bare hand, I can prove this!"

6. Quickly straighten all your fingers. The band will "hop" onto your middle and index fingers. Finish by saying "There you have it, ladies and gentlemen—the hopping rubber band!"

7. After the trick, remove the rubber band, hand it to someone, and say, "You can try this at home. Let me know how it turns out."

11

The Brilliant Assistant's Card Trick

OBJECT: Your assistant will amaze all by "guessing" a card that has been picked out by a member of the audience.

What You Need:
- a friend who knows how to do the trick
- nine playing cards
- pencil or wand

1. Put the cards faceup in three rows, with three cards in each row. Your friend will know ahead of time that whatever spot you touch on the center card in the second row will show her the position of the chosen card. The center card is the clue card.

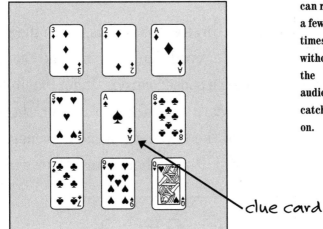

clue card

2. Tell the audience that your assistant will leave the room and that when she comes back, she can identify the card that was chosen.

3. Pick a volunteer to come up and point

to any card. Announce what card the person has chosen, such as the Queen of Hearts or the Ace of Spades.

4. Invite your friend back into the room.

5. With the pencil or wand, randomly touch different cards. But don't touch the center card yet!

6. After three or four cards, touch the spot on the center card that gives her the clue about where the chosen card is. If, for example, the chosen card is in the top row on the right, point to the upper right-hand corner of the clue card. Remember: your helper will know

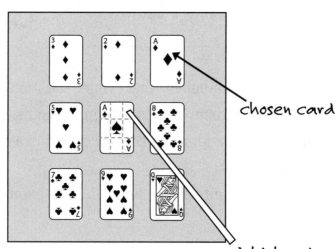

chosen card

upper right-hand
corner of clue card

what the correct card is by the spot that you point to on the clue card.

7. Once she announces the correct card, the crowd will go wild! She should take a bow!

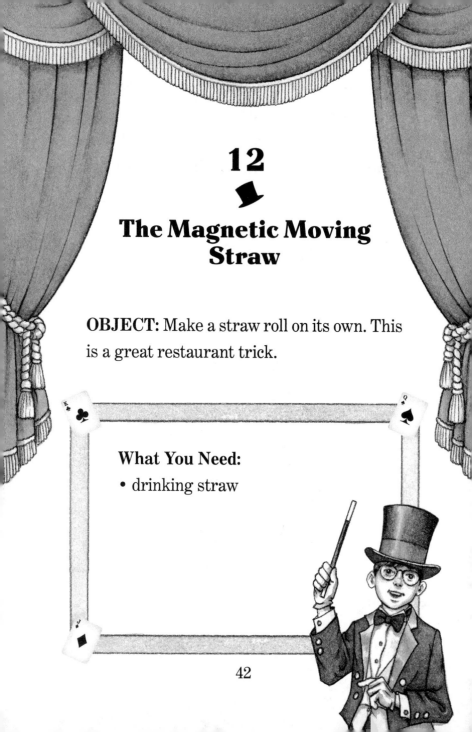

12

The Magnetic Moving Straw

OBJECT: Make a straw roll on its own. This is a great restaurant trick.

What You Need:
• drinking straw

1. Unwrap a straw and place it on the table in front of you horizontally.

2. Rub your hands together and tell the audience that you are creating magnetic currents.

3. Begin moving your finger slowly in circles around the straw. While you're doing this, lean down over the straw as if you're watching it closely for signs of movement.

4. Gradually stop moving your finger and put it in front of the straw. Keep your head bent down over the straw.

5. Begin moving your finger away from the straw, and as you do this, blow lightly on the straw. It will move toward your finger and look as if it's following it.

FACT:
This trick is an <u>illusion</u>. Illusions make people think that they're seeing something impossible, like straws moving or saltshakers floating . . . or magicians floating over sidewalks!

6. You might announce that the magic straw has followed your finger.

13

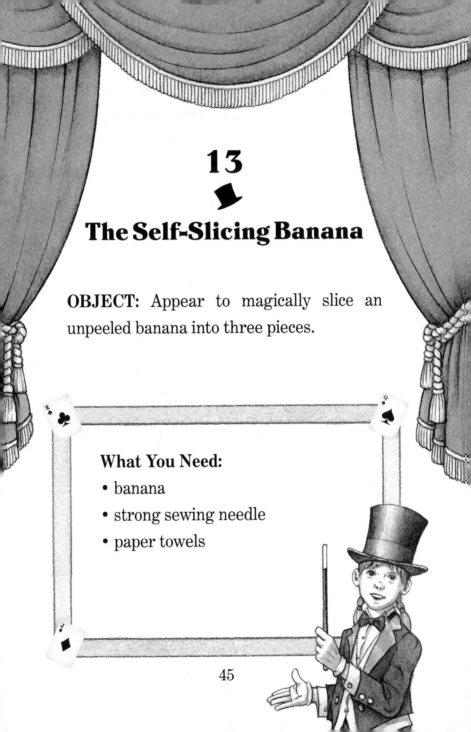

The Self-Slicing Banana

OBJECT: Appear to magically slice an unpeeled banana into three pieces.

What You Need:
- banana
- strong sewing needle
- paper towels

PREPARATION: Before the show, get the banana ready. Push the needle carefully into the top third of the banana until it hits the skin on the other side.

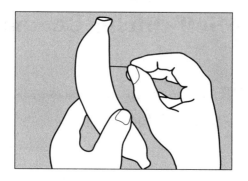

Move the needle from side to side to cut through the banana, but don't make a big hole.

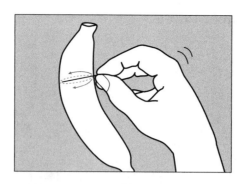

Do the same thing in the bottom third of the banana. This may get messy, so keep a paper towel nearby to wipe the needle and your hands. Rub the holes gently to close them.

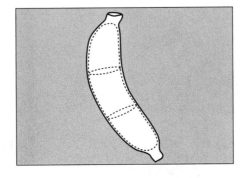

1. Onstage, tell the audience that you can communicate with bananas. Hold the banana up so they can see that it is not peeled.

2. Put the banana down on a paper towel.

3. Speak to the banana and tell it that you need three pieces to share with friends.

4. Unpeel the banana and *ta-da!* The banana seems to have sliced itself!

14

The Balancing Egg

OBJECT: Balance an egg on its end.

What You Need:
- salt
- handkerchief
- egg

PREPARATION: Before the show, put a small pile of salt on the table. Center the handkerchief over the pile.

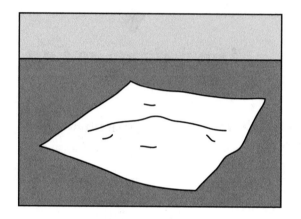

1. Show the egg to the audience and tell them that the handkerchief is there in case there is a mess.

2. Give them a small peek under the corner of the handkerchief to make them think nothing is there.

3. Tell them that an egg can't stand on its own. Demonstrate by trying to balance the

egg on its end. (Make sure it doesn't topple over and break!)

4. Put the end of the egg on the handkerchief and gently press into the salt until it can stand up. You might need some special patter here as the salt could make a crunchy sound.

5. Now step away and let people see the magic!

15

The Disappearing Saltshaker

OBJECT: Make a saltshaker vanish and then reappear!

What You Need:
- coin
- saltshaker
- paper napkin

1. Sit across the table from your audience. Put the coin and the saltshaker on top of the table. Announce that when you tap the coin with the saltshaker, the coin will vanish.

2. Wrap the napkin around the shaker and make sure that the napkin shows the shape of the shaker. (But don't wrap it too tightly.)

3. Hold the napkin with the shaker in it with one hand. Now look hard at the coin, tap it with the shaker, and say, "I command you to disappear!"

4. Look disappointed that the coin is still there. Move the shaker back toward you. Try to make the coin disappear once again. Remember to look at the coin as you pull the shaker back toward your body. Once more, the coin will still be there. You might say, "Rats, this worked last time." Keep looking at the coin!

5. Give it a third try and bring the shaker back toward you even more. When you bring

your hand back, loosen your hold on the napkin just enough to let the shaker fall in your lap. You might patter away as you do this, so the audience doesn't hear the shaker if it makes noise when it lands in your lap.

6. The napkin should still show the shape of the shaker, but the shaker is actually in your lap. KEEP LOOKING at the coin. You don't want the audience to see what's really going on. They'll be looking where you look. You're misdirecting big-time here!

7. Put the napkin (which should still be shaped like the shaker) on the table. Apologize to the audience by saying "Folks, I'm sorry. The coin still seems to be here. To make up for this, the shaker will disappear with my great magical powers."

8. Slap your hand down on the empty napkin, and *presto!* The saltshaker has vanished!

9. Now ask if anyone knows where the shaker is. (They don't.)

10. Say, "Oops! I think it's under the table!"

11. Reach under the table and take the shaker off your lap.

12. Show everyone that the shaker has "magically" reappeared!

16

The Old
Coin-Elbow Wow

OBJECT: Convince people that you've made a coin disappear.

What You Need:
- coin

1. Sit in a chair at the table. Keep your left elbow on the table and your left hand resting on your neck. Tell people that you're going to make a coin disappear by rubbing it on your elbow.

2. Pick up the coin with your right hand and rub it on your left elbow for a few seconds. Rub harder and harder.

3. Look frustrated! After you rub your elbow awhile, drop the coin on the table and tell the audience the trick didn't work but you're going to try it again. Begin rubbing your elbow once more.

4. Drop the coin again, and pick it up with your left hand without missing a beat.

5. Now the coin is in the hand that is pressed against your neck. Quickly begin rubbing your left elbow as if the coin were still in your right hand. Stare hard at your left elbow. You might also mutter that this has always worked before and that you just don't understand what's going on.

FACT:
The first story about magicians was written in Egypt almost 4,000 years ago. It's in a museum in Berlin, Germany.

57

6. Drop the coin from your left hand down your collar while you are rubbing your elbow.

7. Say "Presto!" Then show the audience that both hands are empty.

8. Take a humble bow as the crowd goes wild!

17

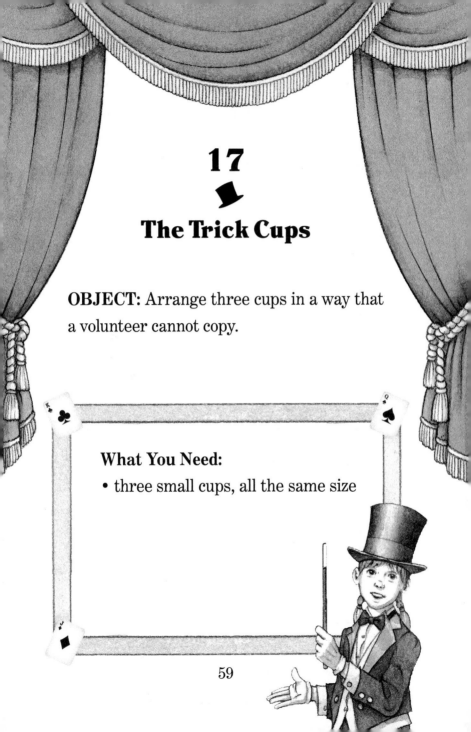

The Trick Cups

OBJECT: Arrange three cups in a way that a volunteer cannot copy.

What You Need:
- three small cups, all the same size

1. Line the cups up in a row from left to right in front of you. The left cup is right side up, the middle one is upside down, and the right one is right side up.

2. Tell the audience that by making just three movements, you can position all three cups upside down.

3. Turn over the left and middle cups.

4. Turn over the left and right cups.

5. Turn over the left and middle cups once again. All three cups will be upside down.

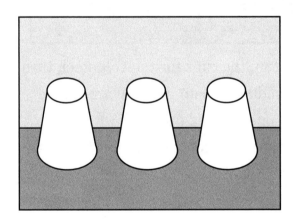

6. Ask for someone to come up and try to do the same thing.

7. Now this is the sneaky part: when you set up the cups for the volunteer, you are going to do exactly the opposite of what you did before. Your audience won't notice.

8. Set up the cups for the volunteer, turning the middle one up and leaving the left and right ones turned upside down.

9. If the volunteer tries to repeat your moves, the cups will all be turned right side up!

10. Shake his hand and tell him better luck next time.

18

🎩

The Unpoppable Balloon

OBJECT: Stick a pin in a balloon without popping it.

What You Need:
- balloon
- clear or invisible tape
- straight pin or sewing needle

PREPARATION: Before the show, blow up the balloon. Put clear or invisible tape on it in several spots.

1. Tell the audience that the balloon will burst only if you command it to.

2. In the spots that you have taped, poke the balloon with the pin. As you do, say, "I command you not to burst." The balloon might make a hissing sound. You could say to the audience that even though the balloon is hissing, the pin can't pop it.

3. Now tell the balloon that you are ready for

it to burst. Stick the pin in a place that you haven't taped.

4. *BANG!*

TRACKING THE FACTS:

You can blow up a balloon because the rubber stretches. If it stretches too far, the balloon will pop. The tape keeps the balloon together so it doesn't pop.

19

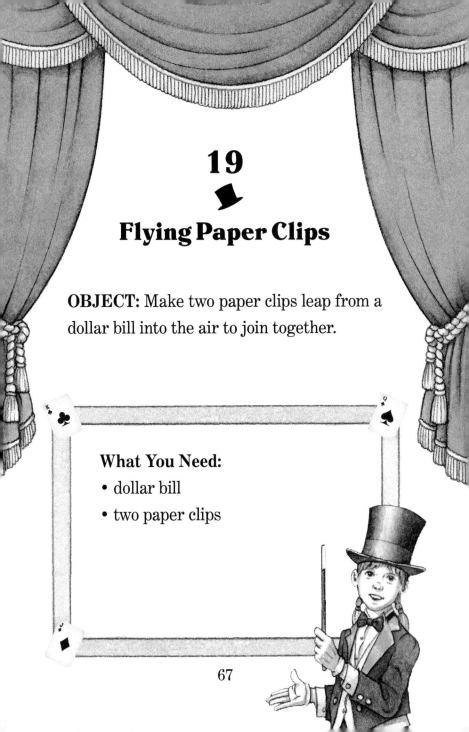

Flying Paper Clips

OBJECT: Make two paper clips leap from a dollar bill into the air to join together.

What You Need:
- dollar bill
- two paper clips

1. Announce that you have found some magical jumping paper clips and will let them perform. Fold the dollar bill in half lengthwise.

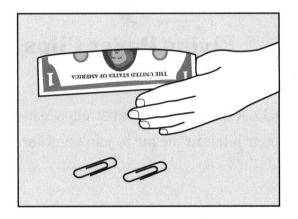

2. Now fold it into the shape of a Z.

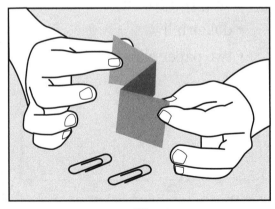

3. Use one paper clip to hold the back and middle of the Z together on the left side.

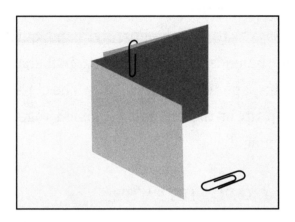

4. Use the other paper clip to hold the middle and top sections together on the right side.

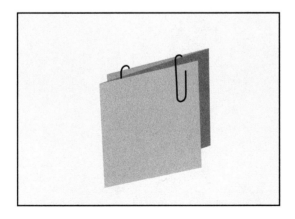

5. Take hold of the bill by each end. Hold it away from your face, so you don't get clipped by a paper clip!

6. Say, "Fly, paper clips, fly!" and quickly pull the ends apart. Be sure to pull sharply so the paper clips can really fly. The clips will jump up in the air and be joined together like magic.

TRACKING THE FACTS:

The way you fold the dollar makes the clips slide down and link together. When you snap the bill quickly, the paper clips will seem to jump in the air and be clipped together.

20

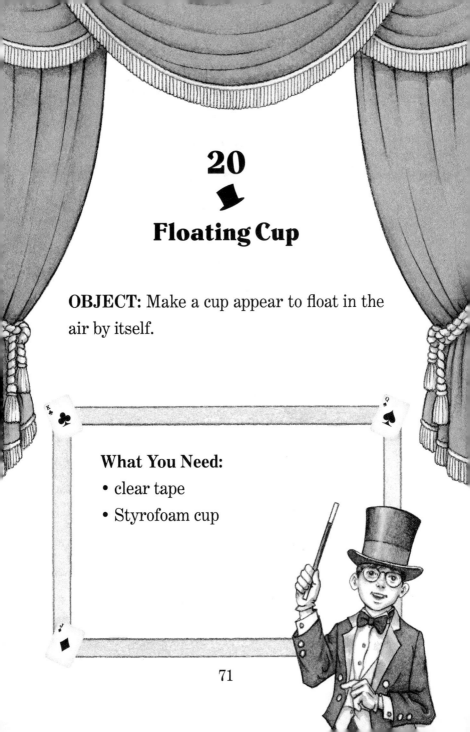

Floating Cup

OBJECT: Make a cup appear to float in the air by itself.

What You Need:
- clear tape
- Styrofoam cup

TIP:
Always
have the
audience
sit directly
in front of
you so they
don't have
a side view
of the
props or
your
hands.
This trick
doesn't
work if
people can
see the cup
handle, so
you'll need
a bit of
distance
between
you and
your
audience.

PREPARATION: Before the show, make a loop of clear tape and stick it to the back of the cup. This should form a little handle just big enough for your thumb to fit through.

1. Hold the cup in both hands with your thumbs in back. Slip one of your thumbs into the loop of tape. Tell the audience that now the cup will magically float in the air.

2. Slowly spread your fingers away from the cup.

3. The cup appears to be floating!

21

The Disappearing
Marble

OBJECT: Make a marble disappear and
then reappear.

What You Need:
- two marbles, beads, or small balls
  that look alike
- paper cup
- scissors

PREPARATION: Cut a hole in the bottom of the paper cup. This can be tricky to do, so have a grown-up help, and be careful with those scissors! The marbles should be able to fit through the hole. You'll want to practice getting them through the hole without looking.

FACT: Houdini's wife, Bess, was his helper onstage.

1. Before the show, put one marble in your pocket.

2. Hold the cup upright in the bottom of your hand.

3. Show the audience that you're dropping a marble in the cup. Tell them that you'll make the marble disappear.

4. Let the marble fall through the hole at the bottom. Keep the marble hidden between the cup and your hand.

5. Now turn the cup upside down, still hiding the marble in your hand. Announce that the marble has vanished.

6. Say that this particular marble was your very favorite one and you hope it's not lost forever. Then, with your other hand, pat your pants pocket and say, "Wait just a minute. What's this?" Take the hidden marble out of your pocket.

22

Superstrong Heavyweight

OBJECT: Seem to make your body so heavy that two volunteers can't lift you.

What You Need:
- two strong kid volunteers

1. This trick has two parts. First you are going to show everyone that it's easy for two people to lift you up. Call for two strong kids from the audience.

2. Ask them to stand on either side of you. Bend your arms at the elbow, and place your left hand on your left shoulder and your right hand on your right shoulder.

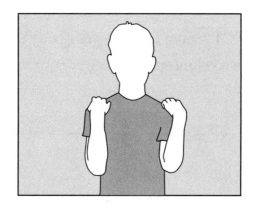

3. Next ask the volunteers to try to grab you under your elbows and lift you up. They should be able to do this easily.

4. Show the audience your biceps and say that now you feel stronger and that you must

have gained about twenty pounds in muscles in just a second or two.

5. Put your hands on your shoulders as you did before. But this time, move your hands close to your neck. Ease your elbows out in front of you. Try to do this in one smooth move.

6. Ask the volunteers to try again to pick you up by your elbows. Impossible!

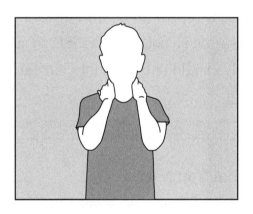

TRACKING THE FACTS:

By moving your elbows forward and away from your body, you've changed your center of gravity. The farther someone gets from the center of your body, the harder it is to lift you.

23

🎩

Really Silly Leg Trick

OBJECT: Appear to be missing a leg—but of course you're not. This trick is so silly you probably should only do it for your family.

What You Need:
- pair of oversized shoes that you borrow from an adult
- coat, towel, or sheet that will cover you from waist to toe

1. Gather the family and announce that you can make one of your feet disappear.

2. In your bare feet or in socks, step into the large shoes you've placed in front of you.

3. Cover yourself from your waist down to your shoes with the cloth. (Don't let your feet show.)

4. Now very carefully, in one smooth move, take one foot out of the shoe and bend your leg at a right angle behind you. (This requires great balance and practice.)

5. If you wobble a little, make it part of the act. Say, "Yikes! It's really hard to stand up with just one foot!" Slowly pull the cloth up. People will see an empty shoe but no foot. (Your other foot, however, will look perfectly normal.)

6. Now slowly lower the cloth, straighten out your leg, and put your foot back into the shoe.

7. Remove the cloth and tell everyone that you're so relieved . . . your foot has re-appeared! YAY! If your parents groan, say, "I'm just a kid, but that was one great FEAT of magic!"

24

The Disappearing Dime

OBJECT: A dime will disappear after you rub it on your hand.

What You Need:
- dime

1. Show the dime to the audience and tell them you can make it disappear simply by rubbing it on your hand. The audience should be directly in front of you.

2. Put the dime on the back of your left hand and begin rubbing it slowly up and down with your right hand.

3. After you do this awhile, drop the dime on the floor. Pretend this is an accident.

4. Lean over and slip the dime in your shoe, but act as if you have picked it up.

5. Say you're going to try making the dime disappear for just a few more seconds and if it doesn't work, you'll admit defeat. Act as if you're returning the dime to your left hand.

6. Continue rubbing it (but it isn't there!) with your right hand.

7. Tell the audience that you need to see if this trick is really working. Lift up your right hand; look amazed and show the audience that the dime has disappeared!

25

The Floating Needle

OBJECT: Make a needle float in a glass of water.

What You Need:
- small drinking glass filled with water
- small piece of tissue paper, about two or three inches wide
- sewing needle
- magnet (if you're feeling especially tricky!)

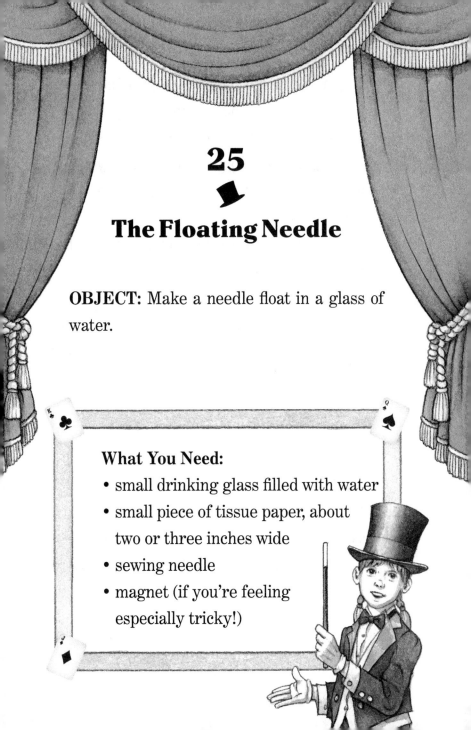

1. Put the tissue paper on top of the water, then rest the needle on the paper.

2. In a short time, the paper will sink. If the paper doesn't sink fast enough, you can gently push it down with a pencil or your wand until it does.

3. Don't touch the needle or glass, and the needle will continue to float.

4. This is a little extra thing you can do: rub one end of the needle with a magnet before you put it on the tissue. It will become a compass!

TRACKING THE FACTS:

The needle floats because of surface tension. The paper sank because it became soaked with water and broke the surface tension.

26

The Hole-in-the-Pocket Trick

OBJECT: A volunteer's coin seems to fall through a different pants pocket than you put it in.

What You Need:
- two quarters—one that is your own and one from someone in the audience
- marker

88

1. Secretly put your quarter on the floor and place your left foot over it. You might try this by dropping a tissue on the floor, and when you pick it up, slide the quarter under your left foot.

2. Ask someone in the audience to bring you a quarter. When she comes up, use the marker to make a little mark on the quarter, and tell her that this way she'll know that the quarter belongs to her.

3. Take the coin and announce that you have a hole in your pants pocket. Put the quarter in your right pocket. Take your hand out and show that it's empty.

4. Shake your left leg and pretend the quarter is falling down your pants leg.

5. While you shake your leg, say, "Wow, this is really strange—the hole must have moved to the other pocket."

6. Lift up your left foot and pick up the quarter that's there. Here's where it gets tricky:

TIP: Because this trick relies on great timing and some acting skills, you'll need nerves of steel. Practice until you've got it down because it's really cool.

Casually put the quarter that you just picked up in your right pants pocket. As you put the coin in your pocket, take out the marked coin that's been hiding there.

7. Look puzzled and ask the volunteer if she gave you the coin or if you were supposed to give it back to her. Let her look at the coin so she sees the mark. Then say, "Thanks so much! Here's your coin!"

27

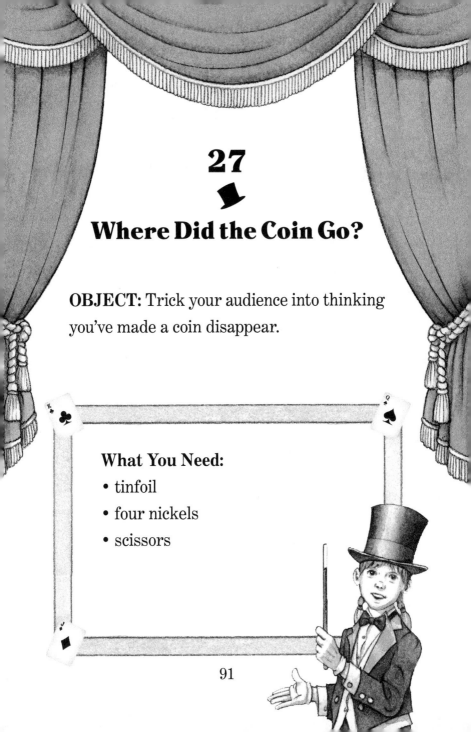

Where Did the Coin Go?

OBJECT: Trick your audience into thinking you've made a coin disappear.

What You Need:
- tinfoil
- four nickels
- scissors

PREPARATION: Tear off a piece of tinfoil that will be big enough to fold around a nickel. Rub the covered coin with your thumb so that you can see a clear outline and the details of the coin underneath. Be sure to do the edges, too.

Now carefully cut out around the coin you've made and *be sure* the sides show. Remove the real nickel. When you finish, the foil should look like a shiny coin.

1. Show that you've got five "nickels" in your hand. Keep the fake nickel slightly hidden by the real ones.

2. Close your hand into a fist. As you do so, crumple the tinfoil coin into a tiny ball with your thumb and push it under the other coins.

3. Open your hand. There are only four nickels. (The fake coin is a tiny ball hidden by the other nickels.)

28

The Ghost Roll

OBJECT: Make a bread roll rise up from the table.

What You Need:
- fork
- bread roll
- cloth napkin

1. Put the fork close to your right hand and the roll on the left side of the fork.

2. Shake out a napkin and place it over the roll and fork.

3. Use your right hand to hold on to one edge of the napkin and the top of the fork handle. Remember, the audience can't see you holding the fork handle!

4. Tell people you need to check to see if the roll is there. Put your left hand on top of the napkin and wiggle the roll back and forth. The roll is under the napkin, but your left hand is on top of the napkin holding the roll.

5. Keep your left hand holding down the roll under the napkin. Push the fork into

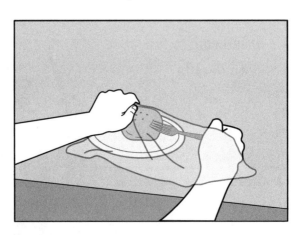

the roll as you patter on about making sure the roll is still there. Look at your left hand the whole time. Grip the fork with your right hand.

6. Hold the left corner of the napkin with your left hand. Say a "magic" phrase, like "Ghost of the roll, arise and show us you're there."

7. As you do this, slowly move the fork up so the roll appears to be rising by itself.

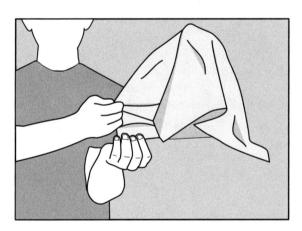

8. As you finish, let the roll fall down to the table. Put your left hand under the napkin to

hold the roll in place. Pretend you're trying to keep it from rising again.

9. With your right hand, whisk the napkin and the fork off of and out of the roll. Quickly put the fork in your lap. And that, ladies and gentlemen, is that!

29

Bread Roll Eats Coin

OBJECT: "Find" a coin inside your roll.

What You Need:

- bread roll
- coin

1. Begin this trick with a bread roll in front of you. Slip a coin into your hand and hold it in a *finger palm*. The audience shouldn't know that it's there.

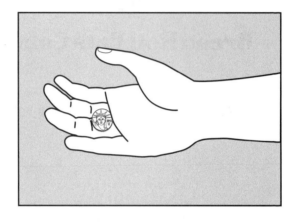

2. Stare hard at the roll and pick it up in your other hand. Shake it and hold it to your ear as if you are trying to listen to something. You might say that you thought you heard something jingling in there.

3. Take the roll in both hands, but keep the coin in the same position. Put your thumbs on top of the roll.

4. Break the bottom of the roll open with your fingers and quickly push the coin inside the bread.

5. Make sure that you hold the roll together so the coin doesn't fall out.

6. Now say, "Yikes, I don't believe this, but there seems to be something in my roll!"

7. Pull the coin out and say, "*Now* I know what was jingling inside the roll! This is better than going to the bank!"

30

Water in the Upside-Down Glass

OBJECT: Make water stay in a glass even after you turn it upside down.

What You Need:
- scissors
- several sheets of paper
- small drinking glass
- pitcher of water
- large pot to catch spilling water

PREPARATION: Cut the paper into three circles that are about an inch wider than the mouth of the glass.

TIP:
It's best to do this trick in a place where spilled water won't ruin anything. Maybe do it outside on a really hot day!

1. Invite someone up to try the trick.

2. Hold up the paper and the glass and say that with the help of a piece of paper, you will keep the water in the glass when it's turned upside down.

3. Fill the glass from the pitcher. Don't fill it quite to the top.

4. Ask the volunteer to put a piece of paper over the top of the glass. Tell the volunteer to hold the glass over the pot and turn it upside down. When the volunteer tries this, the water will spill out of the glass and into the pot.

5. Ask her to try again. The same thing will happen. (Be sure you keep one piece of paper dry for your own use.)

6. Pour water in the glass again. Make sure

the glass is on the table, not in your hand. Fill the water to the very top. Then put a dry piece of paper over the glass. The water at the top will wet the paper. This is what is supposed to happen . . . don't worry!

7. Pick up the glass. Gently and slowly turn it over, but keep your hand on the paper that is covering the glass. Say, "I command you to stay in the glass!"

8. Carefully take your hand off the paper. The water will stay in the glass!

TRACKING THE FACTS:

When the glass isn't completely full, the air inside the glass pushes against the paper with more force than the air pressure, pushing the paper down. When the glass is filled to the brim, no air remains in the glass, and the water can't escape. Wet paper seals the glass tightly, and air can't get in to push the water out.

31

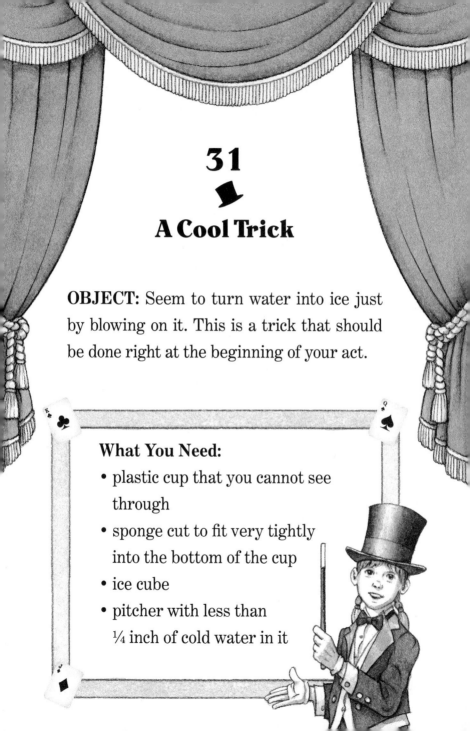

A Cool Trick

OBJECT: Seem to turn water into ice just by blowing on it. This is a trick that should be done right at the beginning of your act.

What You Need:

- plastic cup that you cannot see through
- sponge cut to fit very tightly into the bottom of the cup
- ice cube
- pitcher with less than ¼ inch of cold water in it

PREPARATION: Before the show, push the sponge down into the bottom of the cup so that it's very snug and won't fall out. Put the ice cube on the sponge.

1. Tell the audience that your breath comes from the North Pole and can freeze water.

2. Pour the water into the cup.

3. Blow into the cup as the sponge fills with water. All the water should be absorbed into the sponge.

4. Turn the cup over. The ice cube will fall out!

5. Now say, "Wonder if my breath would help stop global warming!"

32

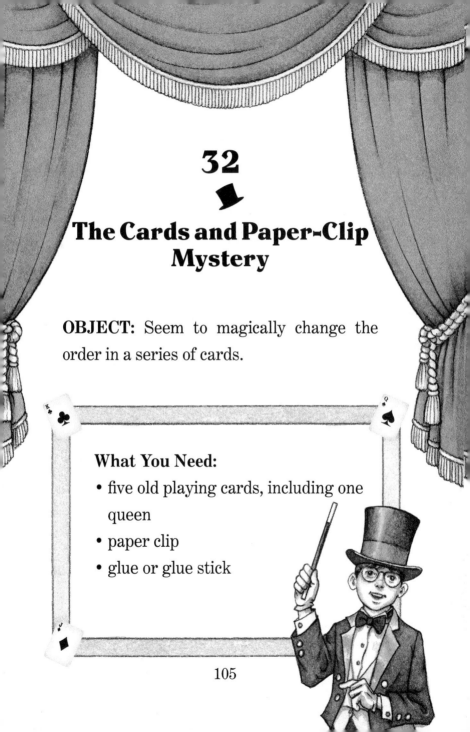

The Cards and Paper-Clip Mystery

OBJECT: Seem to magically change the order in a series of cards.

What You Need:
- five old playing cards, including one queen
- paper clip
- glue or glue stick

PREPARATION: Spread the cards out in a horizontal row, with the queen in the middle. Glue the left sides of the cards together so they look like this:

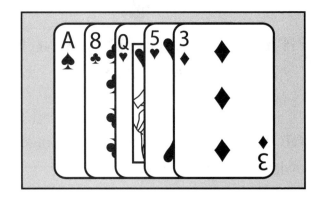

1. Hold the cards up so the audience can see what they are. Call for a volunteer. Ask him to point out which card is in the middle. It should be the queen. Then have him tell the audience what the card is.

2. Now turn the cards to face you.

3. Ask the volunteer to put the paper clip on the center card.

4. Turn the cards back toward the audience.

5. The paper clip will NOT be on the queen. When the cards are turned, people will think that the order has changed. It hasn't. You've created an illusion that's fooled everyone!

33

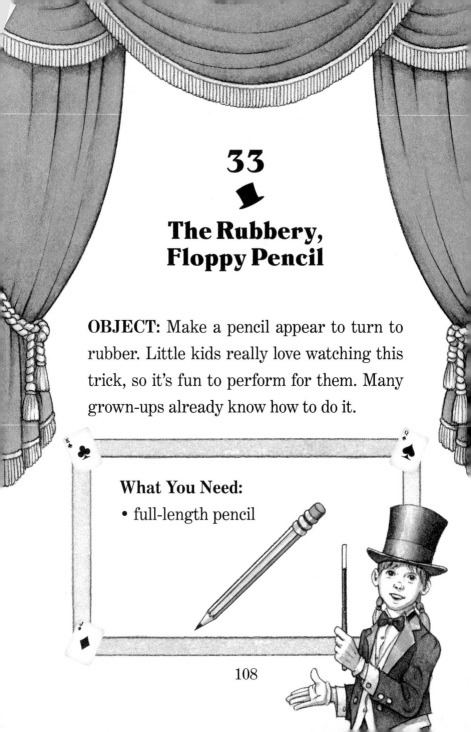

The Rubbery, Floppy Pencil

OBJECT: Make a pencil appear to turn to rubber. Little kids really love watching this trick, so it's fun to perform for them. Many grown-ups already know how to do it.

What You Need:
- full-length pencil

1. Hold the pencil very loosely between your thumb and first finger.

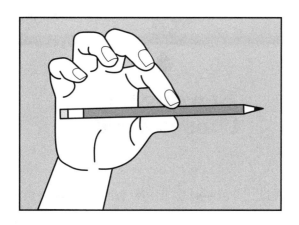

2. Begin shaking the pencil up and down . . . keep a loose grip! Instead of shaking with your hand and wrist, put your whole arm into it and shake more from your shoulder and elbow.

3. You don't have to shake the pencil up and down quickly . . . practice doing it slowly. When you master the timing, the pencil will appear to be soft and floppy as it goes up and down.

TIP:
Take a list of the tricks you're doing with you when you give a performance so you don't forget any. An index card for each trick is great. When you finish a trick, put its card on the bottom of the pile.

34

Sensing the Chosen Card

OBJECT: Pretend to know which card a volunteer has chosen by "sensing" the card she touched.

What You Need:
- deck of cards

PREPARATION: Have the whole deck facing down. Turn one card faceup and place it on the bottom of the deck. It will be the only card that is faceup.

TIP:
It's a good idea to start and end your shows with your very best tricks.

1. Spread out the cards on the table like a fan, still facedown. Make sure that the bottom card doesn't show. Push a few cards over it so the audience doesn't see it.

2. Ask a volunteer to come up and pick a card. As she does, pick up the remaining cards. Tell her to show the audience the card that she's chosen. You are not supposed to see the card, just the audience.

3. As the volunteer is showing the card, turn the deck over in your hand. Do this in a relaxed, sort of cool way that is not obvious. Now all the cards are faceup, *but* (and this is important!) the top card is now facedown. The audience will think that all the cards are facedown. To pull this off, make sure no one

can see what you're doing from the side.

4. Tell the volunteer to put her card face-down in the middle of the deck. Here's the neat part: the volunteer doesn't know that her card and your top card are the only ones that are facedown.

5. Hold the deck behind your back. While it's hidden behind your back, turn your top card over. Then turn the whole deck over so that NOW the volunteer card is the only card faceup in the entire deck. Say, "I have the power to sense her card even though I'm not going to look at any of the cards." Pretend to be thinking hard . . . put your hand up to your head and tap your temple . . . act as if you know everything!

6. After a little more patter, tell them you've sensed the correct card. Lay the deck facedown on the table. Fan out the cards again. Say, "Wow! This is it! I turned her card around so she could find it!" Show the

volunteer the only card that is faceup in the deck.

7. Ask the volunteer to show the card to everyone. The audience goes wild!

35

The Pen Cap Snapback

OBJECT: You "magically" make the cap of a pen snap right back on.

What You Need:

- pen with a cap on it

1. Take the pen out of your pocket. Grumble that you always lose the cap, but you think you've solved the problem.

FACT: Houdini was an expert at getting out of handcuffs and chains. It was said that there was no lock he couldn't open.

2. Secretly wet the index finger and thumb on one hand. You might do this by pretending to be thinking and putting your hand up to your mouth, then giving the two fingers a quick lick. Or have a little cup of water on the floor hidden by a cloth on the table.

3. Hold the pen vertically. Take the cap off and hold it an inch or two above the pen between the two fingers that you moistened.

4. Squeeze the cap between your two wet fingers. It'll shoot back down in place on the pen as if some magnetic force has snapped it back.

5. Do this several times. This is a trick where you can break your "never more than once" rule.

Tips for More Reading

When we were doing research for this book, we read a lot of books and visited a lot of websites. If you want to learn more about magic tricks, check out these books and sites:

- *52 Cool Tricks for Kids* by Lynn Gordon
- *Kids' Magic Secrets: Simple Magic Tricks & Why They Work* by Loris Bree
- *Magic Tricks for Kids: The Ultimate Guide for a Child Illusionist* by G. Allen
- *Usborne Book of Magic Tricks* (Magic Guides series) by Rebecca Heddle and I. Keable-Elliott
- kidzone.ws/magic
- magic.about.com/od/Easy-Magic-Tricks-for-Kids/tp/Magic-Tricks-For-Kids.htm

Have you read the adventure that matches up with this book?

Don't miss Magic Tree House® #50
Hurry Up, Houdini!

The magic tree house whisks Jack and Annie away to the amusement park in Coney Island, New York, to look for Houdini, the famous magician. But for the first time, an argument between the brother and sister puts the mission at risk. Will Jack and Annie be able to see eye to eye in time for Houdini's magic show? And will they get to do some stage magic themselves?

Magic Tree House® Books

Magic Tree House® Fact Trackers

More Magic Tree House®

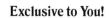